Gallery Books
Editor Peter Fallon

THE TIME BEING

John FitzGerald

THE TIME
BEING

Gallery Books

The Time Being
is first published
simultaneously in paperback
and in a clothbound edition
on 24 June 2021.

The Gallery Press
Loughcrew
Oldcastle
County Meath
Ireland

www.gallerypress.com

ISBN 978 1 91133 808 6 *paperback*
     978 1 91133 809 3 *clothbound*

A CIP catalogue record for this book
is available from the British Library.

The Time Being receives financial assistance
from the Arts Council.

Contents

First Cut *page* 11
First Lesson 12
Seeing Clear 13
Easement 14
Études 15
Spring Thrushes 16
Pond Field Pond 17
Heritage 18
Hen Boy 19
Sisters 20
Light Itinerary 21
Ecstasis 22
Moviddy 23
Scuffle 24
Your News 25
1 WTC 26
While Walking in the Armstrong Woods 27
Disappearance 28
Pact 30
Xuhui 31
At the Jade Temple 32
The Collectors 33
Down Under 34
Velvet Horn 35
God's Pocket 36
Rebus 37
The Island 38
The Dark Edge 39
Post-Socratic Disorder 40
Return to Work 41
Valley Bachelors 42
Lear in Lissarda 43
Augury 44
Adolescence 45
Tree Creeper 46

The Time Being 47
Husbandry 48
All Souls' Eve 49
Breaking Point 50
A Line on the Shore 51
Spindle 52
Fields 53
Fota with Jerry 54
Who 55
Total Recall 56
Epilogue 57

Notes 59
Acknowledgements 60

THE TIME BEING

First Cut

Nothing more heroic for a boy
than a working chainsaw: the smoky
up-throttling roar, spray of dust ejecting,
strain and strength and fixed eye of the holder,
the sweet whiff of danger in exchange
for raw power. It was like cutting into pure fear
to sunder it, then smaller bits so that
it could never grow in the same place again.
And, when he refilled the empty tank
straight from the petrol can, you would stand,
your ears resounding a distant growl,
and watch that old riddle of capacity and bore
play out, as if this was what you had waited
all day for: the *glup glup glup* becoming pour.

First Lesson

Songbirds, flying at first light,
can finish themselves
against the solid air of these panes.
And when they do
the whole house shudders.

At least this wintered thrush,
still warm and opal-eyed,
speckled breast rusting up to the loosed neck,
sprung claws now uselessly fierce,
can have its removal
in the hands of two children.

They whisper rapt exchanges,
grief eased by discovery,
held perfection, privilege of touch;
they don't need to question yet
the sudden brutal instant
when everything and nothing stops
and who and what you were
is of no consequence to the brightening day.

Seeing Clear

This sunny spring morning
the full throttle of a passing tractor
will draw one of them running out
to stare down at the gap between the piers,
wait for the flash revelation: whose tractor it is
and what they're up to on a Sunday.

And, sure enough, I see him
standing on the mown lawn
in his favourite white-hooped jumper,
hand raised to shade his eyes,
brown curls catching at the tips
a glint of auburn from the sunlight.

He turns and waves to me, and I wonder
if my real purpose in returning here
has been to make good the past,
ensure that someone gets it right this time
so that, even if only for an instant,
this much can be clear.

Easement

Spring's other gift
is the illusion of youth.

Today, still in recovery, I sit
on the front terrace, a generous

glass in hand, to hear the birds sing
vigorous as fiddlers — and give up

all my senses to the song
of every bird of Ballymichael,

Dunisky, Crossmahon, Warrenscourt,
all the way back to Kilbarry

where the quick ticking of a wren,
with the insistence

of Mossie Brady's polite poetic stammer,
silences everything.

Études

All day the hiss, the press, the *yess*
of sycamores in first fresh leaf,
as if welcoming themselves, as if melting the wind
passing through them. And, now that I listen,
the ongoing arachnid whine
of harvesters laying down swathes
somewhere around Kilbarry,
a first cut dry for the blade at last.
Just there, the score of a car
along Beamish's Line. And like heartbeat or breath,
always in the inner ear, the songbirds
chiming and half-rhyming
their memes and old motifs and oblique
herewiths and whynots and what'smorebesides.

Spring Thrushes

Where they winter we can't be sure.
There is the science, but that's no answer.

And how do they know just when to come
on to the lawn from the kitchen wood?

So perfectly pointed and preened,
sprung just right for flicking away leaves

and drilling under, locking stock-still
every half-minute, beak-strings wriggling?

Another hop-skip forward. A pause.
Their day has come, and they're having all of it.

Pond Field Pond

Meanwhile surely there must be something
to say for the Pond Field pond.

A discarded shield
landed in a fringe of reeds,

bypassed by heron and swan,
visited only by the occasional mallard or teal.

It's shallow,
but never runs dry.

It's always there — but never at the centre
or the end of anything.

Not worth the bother
of rod or sail or makeshift raft,
or even the attention of the amateur naturalist.

So well hidden from the road
by the hedgerow, nobody knows it's there.

Even the sheep and cattle pay no heed,
grazing their lives away.

Heritage

The slate that lay on the lawn all winter
sank slowly under clover, silverweed,
plantain, the wet grass fringing it unevenly.
I hoped no one would step there
to relish the dull flat snap
and its collapse into two or three spalls,
no longer clean slate
but resigned for reuse on the path
far from the snug slot it once
slid to, fixed to the rafters of the loft
now gone, like the men who built and kept it
stocked, the oats they spilled from the hefted
sacks, the invisible grain-rustling rats, the mill
that winnowed my life into this existence.

Hen Boy

It's how he handles animals that matters most
to him. Gallivanting yesterday, we came across
a racing pigeon crash-landed in a stream,
neck unscrewed from the swollen body, ringed
legs mangled, but the eyes still bright —
so he thumbed them closed for good, deaf to our disgust;
the two escaping frogs I stopped the mower to point
out to him, how he tracked down each
among the docks, homing them both
into open-hearted hands — just as all the hens
ran amok when *Whitey No-name* speared a third
and paddled off, jelly limbs limply flapping,
the others bearing down in hot pursuit, and he
whooping at all creation, like the circus-master's son.

Sisters

Her elopement lasted only seven days
and, on return, she was amazed
nobody would mention it;
it was as though they too had been illicit

in their ways, agreeing not to relate
how someone had turned in the gate,
strolled up the avenue, wouldn't call
or knock but came straight through the hall

singing and dancing and being
open in ways they had never seen,
making his bed among them too —
each one succumbing to his clever lures,

until they realized he couldn't stay: this artful lover
would never match their love for one another.

Light Itinerary

Only the backside bulb of the walking man
is flashing

as though his phone's on silent
in his back pocket

ringing, or he's left the flashlight app set
to strobe.

Slightly stooped, one arm extended,
he seems

a lone backpacker, tramping city crossings,
parks,

like the other trolley-hauling homeless
who are everywhere here,

their eyes avoiding
yours avoiding theirs —

as if to say:
Go, don't go, go, don't go, go.

Ecstasis

If there is
to have been one
moment, it could be this:
body sprung from turf, suspended,
ash-stick hoisted, level and at bay,
arm aloft to pluck a rough-seamed purse
of rag and yarn and glory from the sky;
that instant, every inch of body
and mind outstrained to reach for
the impossible when, into my
hand, like a bird
it came.

Moviddy

Once a good living of rectory and vicarage,
tithes of five-hundred pounds,

the chapel in the early English style
now sprouting this great sycamore trunk

that strains through the open chancel
to congregate with the giant yews outside.

Everything a homily might need
to counsel greater care for our holy places,

if we're to rise again. But we're inured
to plundered tombs, subsiding graves,

ivied headstones listing under
names of substance: the useful high

and mighty Bridges, Walls, and Baileys,
all brought down to earth by age or ailment.

Scuffle

Clouds in their flapping grey tunics
try to hide the lunatic away, out of sight,
an embarrassment to the sky.

Soon, the madman breaks free
to leer at us through all his worn pretences —
old bolete, hoary gewgaw, demi-gourd.

Your News

Something big
has shifted below ground
or ruptured above the clouds
to raise the museum railings even higher,
lengthen the streets and narrow the pavements
crammed with those who couldn't all have known
today was Mercury's day in the sun,
holly blues these exotic leaves
floating through the scomfish air of W1
soon to be rinsed by heavy rain failing
to lighten the weight of sky or centre
the slid cargo still lodged below
so I might walk again without fear of falling.

1 WTC

A schoolyard in Tribeca, mid-morning,
mid-winter, shrill cries swarming like gulls
around a tall figure assenting with a smile
to take each rubber ball and punch it
with the top of a piston fist,
high up into the air, up
where the children's faces follow their eyes rising
beyond fist, beyond head, beyond steel school roof
to each ball at its dependable point of fall,
and indifferent to the continued upward going
of this glimmering glass backdrop to it all,
this one thing that one day will become for them
everything that is impossible and beyond reasonable reach,
like the first unexpected sight of the rest of their lives.

While Walking in the Armstrong Woods

Mischief in the branches high above —
no, worse than mischief: the fell scream
of a marauder, a victim's strangled cries
in a life and death struggle we both
stop to imagine from below. I take in
your singlet-flattened chest, tanned
neck, golden hair, the earnest angle
of your head, and a small grey chick's
feather floating past to land unseen
on your shoulder. I wait for you to act —
shake, itch, brush off the burden,
until I realize this, after all, after all the waiting,
is the real world, the here and now,
the unexceptional quiddling it.

Disappearance

Close to the ridge
    between Thingvellir and Borgarnes,
    she motioned to stop,
        got out,
and walked across a lava track

to one of the drifts familiar from our long approach

    to force her hand into the snow —

    an iron-cold clasp
        she knew would loosen,
    if her warmth would hold.

❖

A hidden thaw gulped uneasily.

    It grew too cold,
    and she withdrew.

❖

Farther down the pass,
the looped-square sign and engraved plaque
    of KROSSLAUG
       tempted us into
cover of birch, past fractal rocks

to a clear-eyed pool
    steaming in spring sunshine.

❖

Still without speaking,
she undressed,
slid under.

Pact

Some nights I dream I am walking
the postglacial tundra with you

somewhere
between Orsk and Orenburg.

We are expecting to be collected
but don't want to be met too soon.

Your bony hand in mine is frail
and precious as found eggshell.

We consider the willows, veil
their catkins in our warm breath,

regard the majesty of the moraines
with proprietorial calm.

You in your navy school uniform,
me in my old leather jacket, long hair.

I already know that when they take you
from me, smile their kind goodbyes,

I must travel the ice-road again
to find you here. But I am calm and sure

because your hair is the same colour
as our foot-printed snow, your eyes

the same pale, unflinching blue
of my determination to return for you.

Xuhui

Down here
the plane trees are newly planted,

well braced with bamboo and fresh rope.
The sparrows are livelier, lighter,

the sky more expansive,
the river chamfered by a kindlier wind.

A white kite lazily figures-of-eight
over low multicoloured turbines.

A tug, its shoulder to the keel, nudges
steadily another steel hulk upstream.

At the Jade Temple

1

Even now I still can't tell if you knew
what to expect that hot July morning
when we visited the Jade Temple. Your
composure unsettled me — like something
learned, or someone inured to nonsense
of the sort that takes and turns vacant minds
against those who can't accept *their* tenets.
Anyway, in the crush, you fell behind
while I was torn and thrown like the joss paper
that fed the courtyard furnace flames;
I sought each Buddha in every chamber
as you quartered and composed your frames
out in the courtyard, circling the fire
that burned my words of devotion, and desire.

2

Yet the images that persist are not those
you recorded: cauterized beggar-wounds,
a young monk reading the paper
as his civilian-on-earth collected petitions
with cash, carved jade Buddhas for sale,
and ghost money available everywhere.
Just as the traders had turned the temple
into a frenzied, chaotic bazaar,
profit seemed everywhere too obvious.
But, maybe that's what we're all in for:
that whatever you gain in this life
not a cause for guilt — just some more
to give to those who choose to barter
for our time in the here-ever-after.

The Collectors

While she slept on he would gather up
the bursts of birdsong around her window,
the whipbird's hiss-cracks from the edge
of the rainforest, a morning star,
as one by one they all pulled out
to follow the bright space-station of their dreams.

During the day there would be eucalypts standing
like beasts of burden in the solid heat,
the tremor he felt when she'd say the word creek,
lorikeets rocketing through street trees
and, once, the draw and sigh of evening sea
as she pressed close to him, whispering her dream
of the leaf-thin eel tonguing its way
through the rocks of the waterfall pool.

Later he would empty his pockets,
adding to the seed-pods, prize shells, found
stones in her basket on the bookstand,
and wait for when she might take it down,
carry it out to the veranda, tip everything
across the sandy table-top
and examine each piece carefully,
her face glowing in amber candlelight,
then replace them all slowly, one by one,
her own particular way.

Down Under

Bushfire smoke trails in a loosening grey
helix from Springbrook down over the city
and out to sea. Evening light fading,
a mauve horizon over graphite sea — fading
fast as I bowl along Hedges. The *Hi Ho! Sold*
sign catches my beams as I pass. A jolly roger
winks from a shady balcony. Two mynahs
scrap noisily in the casuarinas. The lights of Q1
flash, flicker and fix on blue. The rhythm
of the speed-ramps rocks and settles. I am
so far down now and away from it all
that I mustn't lose sight of the sky, keep
my bearings, be sure to come back up
carefully so it isn't all blown in one go.

Velvet Horn

Back home again,
I find another life in liverworts, lichens, ferns,
 at Esknamucky and around the bay
 and talking with you all the while.

I paint and write and botanize a good deal
in the dark hours — mine and theirs,
 and there is always the bay
 and my microscopic finds
 and what the post may bring from you.

Few appreciate that I live
for these exquisite little beauties, my treasures —
 a minor cryptogam subsisting
 among butterwort, alexanders, hungry sundew.

Lately I spent five days admiring just one
and wished often your eye had been in place of mine,
 but was consoled to read
 you had admired my *Ulva verticillata*.

I wish indeed that
 you could visit some of the rocks with me.

I send you this *Fucus tomentosus*,
 knowing it is nowhere near as beautiful
 as what I found.

God's Pocket

Looking from Poulanargid down into Greenville,
the sun still strong
though slipping now from height,
the old chestnut and lime majestic gorged with gold,
and the nap of the meadow
exposing and closing in the warm breeze.

At the top of the valley
huge fashioned paddles rise and disappear
and rise again like giant windblown ox-eye daisies
failing lazily to smite the clouds they chase.

On upwards under Clearach towards Cooldubh,
stopping at the gap to take the view from the Comeraghs
right around to the crooked shark's teeth of the Reeks,
jingling the silver in God's pocket as we go.

Rebus

She is enigma
   out there on the sill,

invisible in black
   against the back

of the night, but for
   two moons,

lime-green,
   lunule-incised,

and when she meows,
   a genital pink

that tongues
   and is remouthed.

The Island

We spared nowhere that day on The Gearagh,
your courage spurring me on to cross
the sunken stretch at the end of the old road
where we could explore the undulating

woodland I had admired so often
from a distance — to discover its hillocks
were just builders' rubble from another time
when that kind of thing was permissible;

and across the mudflats I was always told
would swallow a man whole
I followed your lead, as you would gauge
the hidden depth of step perfectly,

thrilling in the sinking in and hauling out
again; until we reached the island
I had never thought I would find a way
to get to, going into the thicket centre

and calling for you to follow me.
But you just stood out there, waiting,
all light draining into the darkening mire,
as if to say: *you* go on, I will stay

apart now out here, while I have no need.

The Dark Edge

It wasn't a strand
so much as a slope of slippery boulders
giving way to mush

rough underfoot but
softening where the water —
if it was sea water —

pushed at it
with some of the old rhythms
but none of its usual agility.

A small ice floe drifted past
and you joked it was a bear
floating in for the kill.

The only bird we had seen
all week I mistook for
a half-filled plastic bottle

bobbing in the dark oil
that you insisted,
yes, yes, *was* water.

Post-Socratic Disorder

Nothing examines a thing like a hen.
The pigtail post that Nicholas
forgot to de-coop becomes
the main attraction, Exhibit A,
their sidelong strut undoing
as two, three, all lunge in to eyeball
every inch from every angle,
puppet heads flirting out and back,
flushed wattles wobbling
at each novel point of view —
micro-managers, detail sweaters,
two-timing scrutiny with surprise,
fastidious fact checkers wanting to be sure
of no defects in the life worth living.

Return to Work

A very wet day for Julia O'Faolain
and the Marchioness of Dufferin and Ava
to depart. I leave home late
against the pull of having forgotten
something —
again check for wallet, phone, laptop,
as the drag pulls harder
the farther I go along the empty road,
an intergalactic probe trawling
profound space, the absence in my wake
a growing accomplishment of loss,
until everything's gone: the past, my youth,
friends, children, love, home —
and all better off back there without me.

Valley Bachelors

They would drift in, predictable twos and threes,
slowly filling the small room with the week's news,
takes on team selections, name checks, indiscretions.
And you'd forget that beyond the general hubbub
were whole universes of silence —
long lanes, whitewashed yards, bare kitchen tables.
Until once in a summer
the low buttery mid-Cork gobble would unexpectedly pause
and, for that reason, stop;

and each man, embarrassed at having been overheard
or too shy to be the one to strike up again,
would stare down into his glass,
up along the top shelf, at the door — anywhere
for as long as it took for just one voice
to break the enemy's hold.

Lear in Lissarda

You weren't prepared for the void.
Or the interminable length in the day.

Weekend breaks to the same place everywhere
no new museum or local fare could change.

The abrupt subsidence of rage.
Small dissatisfactions gnawed inside

out, leaving pleasure only from the visible:
a shit-stained egg scrubbed up

to an honest glaze, polyps of snow
floating from the high branches

to their mute smash. And all the time,
despite their distance, the persistent

presence of the children, the offending
diffidence of the one who stayed.

Augury

And, halfway out,
we came across a length

of close-woven
rope, floating like

a frond of dried Norfolk
pine, perfectly tubular

and as smooth from use
as the one

some years later
you would loop around

your mother's tree,
then feed through itself

to hold you
at full swing until

as good as could
never be undone.

Adolescence

Trapped between the sashes
and woken by the late winter sun,
you batter at the glass in a complete flap.

I reach in and you take my thumb
in a thready grasp,
upfold your wings and stay
calm until I lift you into open air.

But why not wait?
Why not remain here, at home, where we could
care for you — we would learn how —

rather than breeze around house and wood
for a few glorious hours, playing

with the threat of another hail shower,
and the ominous chill of evening?

Tree Creeper

Now is time for prying, prising,
  when cold finally eases

and bare limbs grow limber
  in the viable air

that incubates titbits for the fits
  and starts of grey-brown

by chance we see scale and swivel
  the sycamores intrepidly,

out of sight now on the far side,
  as if to hide an unlikely white

chest, as if knowing that we too
  will flit to the next distraction.

The Time Being

Now, just before noon,
still morning a few minutes more,

the mist lifts, and the sun comes out,
and the fields beyond the wood are visible,

bright between the trees, making her
sit up from her bolster

among breakfast things, books,
newspapers, notelets, a photograph,

throw back the counterpane, stand
and stretch and walk to the bay

to swing wide the windows, her arms open
to the warmth of the sun returning,

and watch as the last straw bales
are gathered from the paddocks

so that the full extent of the flattest
land can be cleared and free

for her to catch and groom and tack
her sable mare to ride all day

through fresh stubble still harbouring
plentiful grain for the grey birds

flocking to, as she on her mount
striding now holds high her head

in the last warm rays pouring
like silken gold over hair and arms and face.

Husbandry

A handful of liquid air
squirming in a thin plastic sac
from the scales of Twomey's, Back Square —
neither *gabháil* nor *teascán*,
but enough to produce a float-load of hay.

You gauge the range as you broadcast plenty
for the feel of it spending,
trust in the arm's wide sweep and twist
and dying air-drifts to carry them down
like grains of light to settle on the ground
for the tines to work in.

The sowing shouldn't be so easy
and seemingly inconsequential;
the harvest so unending.

All Souls' Eve

The long strokes of the rake draw the leaves in.
They come lightly, easily, still complete
after a dry forbearing autumn.

This, the first leaf-harvest of the season.

I never saw my father use a spade
or rake; his implements were pitchfork
and hedge-shears, though both made him impatient —

he wasn't cut out for their kind of work.

Which is why Jack Gahan came with a scythe
each summer to trim the edges
around the place. We'd watch him lift and glide

the whetted crescent as if it could never falter

in anybody's hands. When we took it
while he rested it fell heavy, crooked.

Breaking Point

We reached there on a switchback
barely visible from the path,
but which I had no trouble finding.
Narrow steps through the pines to an exposed rock
I'd discovered a previous time
gave a comfortable midway view
through trees of the city and sea.
Not much, but enough to reinforce in me a sense
of escape from the ordinary —
yet troubled by your impatience,
how you clipped my observations like your dead-heads.
We wouldn't last more than a short while,
and we didn't —
the city was too close, the summit too far away.

A Line on the Shore

The rhythm of the train riddles through our bodies.
The wind from the opened windows is cool.
The mist has not yet risen,
a sea and her nymphs are sleeping still.

You guess where the train will take you —
you have seen the sunlit buildings at the far end of the bay,
the boats slip into the channel to the hidden town,
ponderous yachts, weary trawlers.
You picture the pier they draw up to;
we were there once, and you can remember everything.

But this train is not going there.
It will take me to another place — near the mouth of the
    channel
where another life is waiting for me on the platform,
leaning into a balcony's shade,
a small bag slung over his shoulder,
a straw hat under his arm, his head angled to hear
our future whisper, whirr along iron tracks
that by noon will be too hot to touch.

Spindle

Each September I scan the hedgerows
    for your gaudy lanterns
    lighting up the green-dark shade:
pink biretta, plump pods, daring orange aril.
But I never find them,

except at the spot on the bank opposite that grim
    breeze-block and pallet-littered place,
    devil dogs still barking at the open gate
I slunk past on my way to school
and home again, sickening.

Lair of the worse-than-useless,
    now skewered in his grave, pig-smelling flesh rotted
    to bone, worms fingering the dumb skull,
made neighbour, tenant, small-farmer, all by
my ignorant father.

One year soon, when I meet courage on the way,
I will gather some of your pegwood litter
    to make a ground-fire, and draw the frail charcoal
    across your smooth bole,
a diamond threaded end to end —
and there will end his tenure.

Fields

There's a place on the Dublin-Cork line
where woodland opens out to fields within the wood —
two or three,
irregular in shape and secretive in their deep surround,
unperturbed by the sudden pulsing passing-through of trains.
And then they're gone.
I always seem to lift my eyes at just this point in the journey,
signalled by some animus of field
and its possession of me since a child,
for all the fields I have traversed
and loved and lost along the way.

Fota with Jerry

Egrets stilting streams, the broken wall of Belvelley Bridge,
its toppled sandstone blocks bruising the dun shallows,
and so many years now since we circumambulated the island,
followed the railway line in search of Townsend's couch-grass
when we should have been in lecture hall or library.

But we weren't made for that. And this was all before the
    by-pass,
wildlife park, hotel, chalets, golf academy. Back then
it was just the shuttered house and unkempt arboretum,
neglected farmland — somewhere entire set aside for our
    diversion,
the thick belt of holm oak and our own awkward bravura
useless holds against all that was to come undone.

Who

A light wind ruffles the river poplars,
rousing me from daydreams of gold and green;
when it reaches here the beech leaves shiver,
then settle back to the season's regime
of warmth and silence and limitless time —
healing a body unused to this pace,
and with nothing to think of but how to find
more time to while away in this place.
It moves through the woods, a secret spoken
by tree to tree, until it reaches the lane,
and from there, or thereabouts, half-woken,
a pigeon croons every now and again:
Who? Who is it? Who-who, who is it?
Who-who, who is it? Who?

Total Recall

Watery snoring of toads in warm dark.
The invisible, unmentionable pet snark

as a child you harboured and still hold to.
That just-about-to-land-anywhere-might-do

flight of the egret across the Huangpu.
'A bearded chap waving from the poop'

as the ferry that carries us bow-waves back.
Donnelly and Gerdy on the Nun Attax —

simian crouch, rough northern burr.
How walking the dawn streets together

was the only time you'd want to sing.
I wish I didn't still remember everything.

Epilogue

after Virgil

These things I rhapsodized: fieldwork, livestock, trees,
as Caesar was proclaiming victory at the Euphrates,

a peacemaker among querulous tribes
on a fast track to stardom.

Meanwhile, I myself found succour in Naples:
O salad days of sweet languid leisure

riffing country tunes for you, Tityrus,
beneath our copious beech.

Notes

page 17   The first line is taken from W S Graham's poem 'The Constructed Space'.

page 26   1WTC is shorthand for the World Trade Center in New York, rebuilt following the terrorist attack on 11 September 2001. At 1,776 feet, it is the tallest building in the Western Hemisphere.

page 35   'Velvet Horn' is based on correspondence between botanists Ellen Hutchins and Dawson Turner and contains a number of verbatim extracts from their letters.

page 48   *gabháil* and *teascán* are agricultural terms in Irish carrying over into Hiberno-English, meaning 'armful' and 'cutting' respectively.

page 56   'A bearded chap waving from the poop' is a phrase from the novel *Bornholm Night Ferry*, by Aidan Higgins, published in 1983. Nun Attax was a punk band of the 1970s and 1980s based in Cork. Band members included Finbarr Donnelly and Giordai (Gerdy) O'Laoghaire.

page 57   'Epilogue' is a translation from Virgil's *Georgics*, Book IV, 559-566.

Acknowledgements

Acknowledgements are due to the editors of the following publications where some of these poems, or versions of them, were published first: *Atlantic Currents* anthology (edited by Paul Marion, Tina Neylon and John Wooding), *Burning Bush 2, Cyphers, The Deep Heart's Core* anthology (edited by Eugene O'Connell and Pat Boran), *Everything to Play For* anthology (edited by John McAuliffe), *The Irish Examiner, The Irish Independent, The Irish Times, Poetry Ireland Review, Quarryman, Reading the Future* anthology (edited by Alan Hayes), *Skylight 47, The Stony Thursday Book, Windharp Anthology of Irish Poetry 1916-2016* (edited by Niall MacMonagle) and *The Well Review*.

Thanks are also due to Patrick Cotter, Director of the Munster Literature Centre and Editor of the Southward Editions *New Irish Voices* Series for publishing my chapbook *First Cut* in 2017, and to Jamie Murphy of The Salvage Press for publishing *Darklight*, a limited edition letterpress printing made in collaboration with the artist Dorothy Cross in 2019. 'Valley Bachelors' was selected as the poem to represent Ireland on the London Underground for St Patrick's Day 2018.

I wish to thank the Directors of the Key West Literary Seminar, Florida, USA; the Artisa Retreat, Epidaurus, Greece; and The Tyrone Guthrie Centre, Annaghmakerrig, Ireland, for opportunities to spend time writing and revising in these places from 2015 to 2020.

A number of poems are dedicated to people. 'Pact' is for Irina-James; 'Seeing Clear' is for Nicholas; 'Adolescence' is for Elena; 'The Island' is for Alexander; 'Valley Bachelors' is for William Trevor and 'Augury' is in memory of Brendan Mulcahy.